Other books by George Grotz

The Furniture Doctor

From Gunk to Glow

The New Antiques: Knowing and Buying Victorian Furniture

Antiques You Can Decorate With

Instant Furniture Refinishing and

Other Crafty Practices

Instant Furniture Refinishing and Other Crafty Practices

George Grotz

"The Furniture Doctor"

Dolphin Books

Doubleday & Company, Inc.

Garden City, New York

Dolphin Edition: 1973
Originally published by Doubleday & Company, Inc.
in 1966

ISBN: 0-385-03628-0

*This book is dedicated to all kindred
souls who have also spent their lives looking
for easy ways out.*

Old Crafty-Eyes —
A Sort of a Preface

Or, how I learned to find 'em, fool 'em, and get out of the house in a hurry!

I HAD a terrible job once. It was right after my first refinishing business went down for the third time. Of course, that wasn't really my fault. It was my wife's Uncle Tom that did it. He was going to help me out. (He helped me out of my business, is what he did!) He was going to show me how to build my miserable little operation into a chain of refinishing shops that would blanket the nation or girdle the globe or something. We were even going to have a mail-order division.

According to my wife's uncle, we would girdle the globe with refinishing shops or something.

Anyway, there I was, broke, and the kids were giving me dirty looks for being a failure. So I had to get a job. I took the second one that I was offered, and it turned out to be this terrible one. It was what you call in the furniture business a "polisher." Now, that does not mean that you polish furniture. That would be too obvious. What it means is that you go around to houses fixing furniture that delivery men have damaged on the way from the department store. Then, after the customers have had the furniture a few years, you go around patching up their cigarette burns and replacing missing pieces of veneer and sometimes even refinishing whole pieces right in their house. Or (and this has a lot to do with this book) *convincing* them that you have refinished whole pieces right in their house.

And believe me, this job was a rat race. It made that time I worked on Madison Avenue look like an old ladies' picnic. Every morning, eleven of us would report to this little office in the Bronx. It was just about at the edge of the city, where the suburbs begin, and if you were smart, you got there just about sunrise. When you arrived, there was this crafty-eyed little guy sitting behind a desk in an office that was a nightmare of 1920 Modern, pale blond squares of wood with black edges and lucite shelves—Early Nothing, as it is called in the trade.

Well, the first morning, Crafty-Eyes takes you down into the cellar to have you refinish a piece on the premises so he can find out if you are fooling him or not.

*There was something about the boss's eyes that should
have tipped me off about the kind of a job it was going
to be.*

Then, if you pass that test, the next morning he gives
you ten or twelve little slips of paper, each listing the
name of a furniture store and its customer's address.
Then, he explains, you go around (in a car that Crafty-
Eyes got financed for you) to all the addresses to fix
whatever is the matter. You're supposed to introduce
yourself as having been sent by the store listed on your
slip, and never mention Crafty-Eyes' service. It was a
sort of Secret Service. For doing this, you get between $2.50 and $3.50 a call, depending on how far
away from the office the houses are. (We had a giant
map on the wall with radius circles drawn on it.)

All of which sounds great when Crafty-Eyes explains

it to you. Say, you can make $35 or more a day. Except
that you can't. Because all these places are about ninety
miles apart and you have to spend three quarters of
your time trying to find them. The result, of course,

*The trouble was that all the places were about ninety
miles apart.*

is that, once you find one of these addresses, you can't
waste much time there, and if there is a quick way
to do anything, you had better find out about it—or
even invent it—if you want to complete more than four
calls a day. The name of that business should have been
"The Find 'Em, Fool 'Em, and Get Out of the House
as Fast as You Can Furniture Polishing Service."

The first day on the road I made $7.50 less $2.85
in automobile and eating expenses, not to mention a
$1.35 can of spray lacquer that I left in somebody's
house by mistake. And when I got home the kids
were crying and the wife was cranky, and I began to
wish I'd taken that first job I was offered, in a coffin
factory. At least it would have paid me a steady $75
a week.

The idea was to get in and get out as fast as you could.

Anyway, the upshot of all this was that on that job I learned from the other fellow and thought up for myself more tricks and shortcuts than were ever thought of before. And I began to get a pretty crafty look around *my* eyes, too. "Sneaky George," they called me after I turned in seventeen slips one day and there were eleven complaints the next day—so that I had to go back to do the jobs over.

One day I made a real killing, because this lady

wanted her whole bedroom set refinished. Now, of course, when you ran into a complete refinishing job you didn't do that for any $2.50 or $3.50. In that case you were supposed to quote the lady a price—as high as you thought the traffic would bear after looking over the general quality of the furnishings in her house. Then you were supposed to call the office from an outside phone, tell Crafty-Eyes the price, and start to work before she changed her mind. The service was supposed to get half of whatever you collected. Of course, some of the fellows used to lie to the boss about how much they were getting, but naturally not me.

Well, in this particular case I didn't really want to do the job because in the first place I hate working on

The author waiting for a live one in front of his shop.

junk, and in the second I had gotten acclimated to racing around the five boroughs of New York City and the neighboring counties of Connecticut and New Jersey. So I quoted the lady an outrageous price—$180 for the three pieces. It *was* outrageous, and she couldn't possibly take me up on it. But she did. And there I was, stuck with her junk.

Well, you can call me a liar if you want, but I'll be darned if I didn't finish her three pieces that same day —and if that isn't instant refinishing, I'd like to know what is! And if you want to know how I did it, you will find out somewhere in the pages of this book. Because, gentle reader, that is the kind of thing that a lot of this book is about: *how to make your furniture look like new and get out of the house fast.*

I hope you find it useful, I really do. I have to say so, anyway, you see, because I'm trying to get rid of that crafty look around my eyes.

Love to you all out there—especially you, lost and gone little Lissa, lost in the wilds of Neptune, New Jersey.

GEORGE GROTZ

Provincetown, Massachusetts
January 15, 1965

Contents

Being a cackle of ways to make your furniture look like new without actually refinishing it. Including cures, placebos, and first-aid for white spots and rings . . . how to make tops alcoholproof and waterproof . . . loose veneers . . . cigarette burns . . . chipped veneers and missing inlay pieces . . . worn spots and edges . . . scratches and gouges . . . black spots and rings.

Find your ailment in this chapter. For each case a treatment is prescribed. Diagnosis: hazy, blushed, or cloudy finish . . . crackled, cracked, or alligatored finish . . . worn and thin finish . . . abused ("really beat-up") finish. Treatment: abrasion, overcoating, reamalgamation, padding. A special note about Danish Modern (or any other furniture with a "sealer" finish).

Maybe not Instant—but fast and easy. It's the sneaky art of Making Something Out of Nothing. Ground coat, decoration, glaze, finishing off, pickled finish.

1. The Gentle Art of Faking Out, or How to Cheat with Class

Being a cackle of ways to make your furniture look like new without actually refinishing it. Including cures, placebos, and first-aid for white spots and rings . . . how to make tops alcoholproof and waterproof . . . loose veneers . . . cigarette burns . . . chipped veneers and missing inlay pieces . . . worn spots and edges . . . scratches and gouges . . . black spots and rings.

ONE approach to Instant Refinishing is sheer trickery and deceit. And, of course, this is the quickest method —when you can get away with it. I mean, lots of things can happen to furniture that make it look awful but that can be corrected or cured without any kind of re-finishing (Instant or Otherwise) at all. I am talking about chips, scratches, white spots, black spots, and that sort of thing. And once these blemishes have been removed, all the piece needs is a rubdown and a waxing to make it look like new.

That this is cheating of the first order, I am well aware. But, as with most of man's activities, it isn't what you do but how you do it. And what I am un-abashedly proposing here is the raising of cheating to the level of an art form. Like painting or sculpture or cooking a pineapple upside-down cake—important things like that.

So let's get on with today's lesson on "faking out." Seriously, there aren't any vast generalities I can give you in this introduction. Each of the ills and cures we are about to discuss is pretty much unrelated to the others. All I can do is to point out that with rare exceptions all the materials needed are commonly available. I have tried to spell things out in what I am afraid may on occasion be insulting detail. But I think it is better to go too far in this direction than to assume anything about what somebody might already know. It is easy for me to forget that people haven't all spent the last twenty years of their lives knocking around furniture-repair shops.

So it seems to me that if you can read and follow directions you should be able to do all these things.

WHITE SPOTS AND RINGS

After the ball is over . . . after the party is done . . . breathes there the heart so cold that to itself has never said, "These are my own, my native rings." White rings, that is. Just the same size as the bottom of a highball glass.

First Principle: All white spots, rings, circles, and Rorschach blots are caused by water molecules uniting with other molecules in the surface of a *cheap* finish. Sorry, but good finishes will not white-spot. If you have a finish that does, and you think it is a good one, somebody sold you a bill of goods. A varnish finish will not white-spot. A sealer finish will not white-spot. Even a *good* factory-sprayed lacquer will not white-spot. The offenders are the *cheap* factory-sprayed lacquer finishes.

In the case of rings caused by drinking glasses, it is a matter of airborne water molecules condensing on the outside of the glass and running down its sides. Or by spillage.

In the case of white spots caused by hot plates, it is not really the heat, but condensation caused by the difference in temperature between the plate and the table—although the presence of heat makes the white spots happen faster.

Now, there is one good thing about white spots, and that is that they almost always look worse than they are. That is because they are on the surface of the finish. They rarely go deeper than the top five percent of the finish's thickness. This means that they can be removed either chemically or by mild abrasion without bothering the ninety-five percent of the finish beneath them that remains clear.

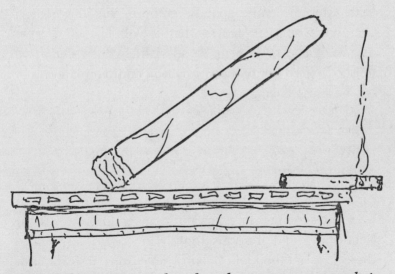

One of them ruins you but the other one cures you, whatever that means.

I think the easiest way to remove white spots is to rub them with cigar ash, wetted to a paste with a few drops of water. That's the way Great-Grandma did it, and it should be good enough for you. But, of course, it doesn't work on all modern finishes, and in that event try ammonia. Don't pour it. Just dampen a small pad of cloth and whisk it over the surface. It is the fumes that do the work.

Or you can wet a pad with lacquer thinner and use that with the same light, barely-touching-the-surface stroke.

Those are the three chemical methods. Abrasion— actually grinding off the top five percent of the finish —should be done with grade ooo or oooo steel wool.

Of course, the trouble with the abrasion method is that, after the white spot is removed, you have to go over the whole surface so that it will have the same degree of sheen. But that's all right. When you have finished, just rewax your surface, and you are ready for business again.

HOW TO MAKE TOPS ALCOHOLPROOF AND WATERPROOF

White-spot proofing has nothing to do with Instant Refinishing, but it seems foolish to leave it out, since there is a method of making table tops resistant not only to water but even to alcohol. And as any antique

lover will tell you, there are finishes that a spilled mar-
tini will remove completely.

Here is what you do. There is no way of treating a
finish to toughen it, and what you have to do is cover
it with a film that doesn't react to either water or
alcohol. At this point somebody always suggests tar.
But that is too sticky and also tends to obscure the grain
of the wood. What we are going to use is something
almost as frightening.

Namely, varnish.

The reason this is so frightening is that I am sure
there breathes no soul who hasn't had trouble with varnish, in the form of bubbles or specks of dust. But
your troubles are over from this day forward if you
hearken to the rules of Grotz and deviate not. If you
follow these rules, you will be able to apply a faultless
coat of varnish onto any existing top and be assured
that it will remain completely alcoholproof and waterproof for as long as it receives normal usage. (You
can't leave it out in your backyard over the winter, for
instance.)

Rule 1: Buy a brand-new two-inch paint brush. No
exceptions. The brush *must* be brand new, and you
can use it to varnish with only once. Also, it must be
an ordinary paint brush of good quality. It will cost
in the range of 85¢ to $1. It *must not* be a varnish
brush. Varnish brushes are for use by experts, and the
amateur will invariably produce billions of those tiny
bubbles.

Rule 2: Buy a brand-new can of furniture or floor

varnish. Either one. They are exactly the same. What you must avoid is *spar* varnish, which is for use out-of-doors. (It is tough, but it stays just a little bit soft so that it can resist extreme temperature changes, and that is no good for table tops.) Never use old varnish. Buy a new pint can for every job.

Rule 3: Buy a brand-new pint can or bottle of paint thinner or mineral spirits, which are the same thing. *Not* pure gum turpentine, which can impair good drying.

Now, the rest of the process is just common sense. But it seems to be very hard to convince people that they *must* buy a NEW brush, NEW varnish, and NEW thinner. This has to be a hard-and-fast rule, and you get no refunds if you don't follow it in all particulars.

The process is as follows:

1. Wash the surface of your table with the paint thinner. Pour on half a cup, scrub it around hard with a soft cloth, and wipe dry with another piece of cloth. Then do it all over again. This will remove all traces of wax. If any traces were to remain, your varnish would not dry.

2. Into a clean soup bowl, pour approximately one cup of your varnish and add about a quarter of a cup of the paint thinner. Don't worry about your varnish being too thin. A thin coat is just as good as a thick one. You are not building a wall, just changing the nature of the surface.

3. Brush this on helter-skelter until the whole surface is covered.

4. Brush the varnish smooth with the tip of the brush, using long strokes that go from edge to edge.

5. Go away and leave the varnish to dry all by itself. If you come back to peek and you see brush marks, restrain yourself and go away again. They will level themselves much better without your help.

6. The next day, scuff the surface with ooo steel wool, using long, light strokes that go from edge to edge, following the grain of the wood.

7. Apply a thin coat of paste wax and polish with a soft cloth.

8. Now you can start spilling things on your alcoholproof and waterproof finish.

LOOSE VENEERS

Loosening of veneers doesn't happen anymore with *good* modern furniture or *good* reproductions of traditional styles, simply because they are made with waterproof glue. Loose veneers are caused by moisture in the air seeping into the old-fashioned fish, hide, and hoof glues, which were terrible.

But the nature of these old glues suggests the easiest way to repair loosening veneers. For, besides softening from moisture in the air, they also soften with the application of heat. So you can *iron* them down.

The best way to do this is to cover the area that is flapping with two sheets of waxed paper. Then add about ten sheets of newspaper and place your iron on top of that. Set the iron at low heat and let it stand there for ten minutes. Take the iron off, and replace it with a big stack of books to hold the veneer down while the glue is cooling and hardening. If any of the waxed paper sticks to the finish, remove it by rubbing the area gently with mineral spirits and ooo or oooo grade steel wool.

This method of tightening loose veneers will work— *if* nobody has gotten there before you. But in the event that someone else has already squirted three or four

This has something or other to do with loose veneers, but I forget what.

kinds of glue under the flap and it won't lie flat, the only answer is to get a brand-new (UNUSED) single-edge razor blade. Using a metal straight-edge to insure clean, straight lines, cut the loose area of the veneer away. Then carefully scrape off the dirt from the furniture and from the underside of the piece of veneer. Finally, glue the piece of veneer back in place with any white glue, covering the area with waxed paper and weighting it down with a pile of books to insure that it dries flat.

You'll be surprised what a neat, hardly visible line you will get by having used a BRAND-NEW single-edge razor blade. And now, to prevent future loosening, you will want to give the whole top a thin coat of varnish. This will seal out the moisture in the air that causes your trouble. For varnishing directions, see the rules in the previous section on "White-spot proofing."

CIGARETTE BURNS

You know, I could tell you how to patch cigarette burns, but the more I think about it, the more I think it would just make you hate me. It would make life too hard for you, you see. The only *right* way to patch cigarette burns is with shellac sticks, which come in 84 colors, and dry powder stains, which come in 124 colors. And after you have bought all this stuff, you have to practice about ten hours a day for two weeks. It's the sort of thing you learn by apprenticing.

It is certainly much easier to call in a professional patcher or "burn-in" man (the stick shellac has to be melted with a hot blade) to do the job for you. And since most people don't even know such practitioners exist, I'll tell you how to find them: they either work full time for big furniture stores—or department stores with big furniture departments—or they run their own service, traveling around to stores that sell television sets and fancy (wooden) record players.

If the man is a full-time employee of a furniture store, he will be glad to come around to your house on a weekend. And being on his side, I would say he should get five dollars for the call even if the job only takes him fifteen minutes. If you have half a dozen burns, he should charge you $5 for the first one and only $2 for each additional one.

Of course, if you find your man by asking at a big television store, the fellow will come anytime you want and will charge you the standard rate for your area.

Of course, if you insist on doing this yourself, buy my other book called *The Furniture Doctor*, which goes into details and tells you where to buy the stuff.

However, if you are the kind of person who absolutely insists on doing things for himself, there are two things that you can do about cigarette burns with comparatively easy-to-find materials.

The first (and easiest) way is to scrape the burned area smooth with a curved blade (such as you find on a jackknife) and then smooth it with a tiny piece of very fine sandpaper. Then you paint the area the same color as the rest of the wood. Artist's oil colors are best, and after you have mixed your exact color match, smudge the paint into the area with your fingertip so that you will have the thinnest possible coat. The reason for this is that a thin coat will dry much faster and harder. Don't thin the paints but use them as they come out of the tubes.

Next, spray the area with one coat of clear plastic spray, and when it is thoroughly dry, spray the whole surface to get an even refraction. Finally, rub it down with fine steel wool and wax it. (See directions for Overcoating on page 48.)

The other way to work on cigarette burns is to scrape the burned area smooth and fill it with colored wax. Dectostick is the best brand I know of, and it is designed for just this sort of work. The process is the same as I describe below for filling holes left by chipped veneer and missing inlay pieces.

CHIPPED VENEERS AND MISSING INLAY PIECES

The easiest things to fix, and the most fun, are chipped veneers and missing inlay pieces. What you do is buy the biggest box of wax crayons you can find and take out all the browns, reds, tans—or, if you have green furniture, all the greens. Anyway, you either find a color that closely matches the color you want in your depression or you mix the colors to get a match. This is done by melting little pieces together in a tablespoon over your kitchen range. (Don't use matches, which would add soot to the wax.) In some places you can buy little colored wax sticks designed for this very purpose. Hardware stores and the stores in front of lumber yards are the best places to look for them, but they *are* hard to find.

Dribble the melted wax, or mash the stick of wax, into the hole. Scrape it flush (first letting the melted wax cool) with a dull table-knife blade.

Now, in some cases, this will look good enough and serve the purpose—say on the face of a drawer or a table edge. But in case you want to finish over it, it is essential to apply a thin coat of shellac first, because shellac

The poor man's patching kit, but it works if you're not in the habit of leaving hot irons on your cocktail tables.

is the only thing that will dry over wax. Incidentally, shellac does come in spray cans. Zinzer has it and probably other companies. After the shellac, you can apply any other spray or even varnish over your wax patch.

WORN SPOTS AND EDGES

Wear, of course, is a matter of degree, but for our purposes we can divide it into two classes:

1. Simple wear, by which I mean merely a dullness of the finish or even the removal of the finish through wear if the wood underneath and the stain in it have not been disturbed. In other words, the area of wear is still the same color as the rest of the surface.

2. Deep wear—meaning that the area of wear is lighter than the rest of the surface because some of the stain has been worn or wiped out of the wood. This happens particularly on the edges of tables made of dark wood.

In the case of simple wear, the solution is easy. Simply coat the whole top with a spray can (see Overcoating on page 48).

As for deep wear, let's start with edges. About the easiest way to restore color to worn edges is to apply iodine or black or brown ink with the side of a small water-color brush. Or you can mix a color that is an exact match by using water colors. When the stain or paint has dried, you simply spray over it to keep it from getting rubbed off.

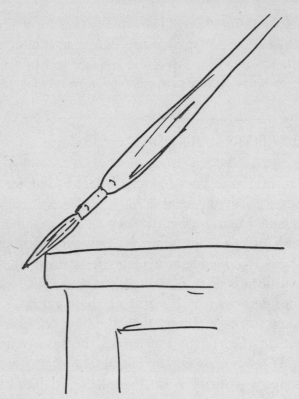

Touching up edges—for people who are diffident about buying good furniture in the first place.

Edges are easy to do, but a deep-wear spot in the top of a table will take some patience. Here, the best thing for the amateur to use is a set of artist's oil paints. You can wipe them off easily with a rag moistened with turpentine and start all over again until you arrive at exactly the color you want. Of course, you can buy separate tubes of the paint. Good basic colors to work with would be burnt sienna, raw sienna, raw umber, burnt umber, yellow ocher, white, and black. That's seven tubes in all.

As to application, you will find that you do much better with a pad than a brush. It is called wiping-on, and the smudging of the paint makes the edges of your job almost invisible. In fact, you will find that by smudging-on the paint with one pad and wiping it off gently with another dry pad you can get incredible results.

Mix the colors without any thinner. You can mix them with a brush, but apply them with a pad. They have to be good and thick if they are to smudge well and thinly.

After the paint has dried thoroughly (three days in a warm room, less in direct sunlight or near an electric heater) apply an overcoating of clear spray-can finish (see page 50).

SCRATCHES AND GOUGES

Fundamentally, you are in as much trouble with scratches and gouges as you are with a cigarette burn, and the best answer is to find a professional patcher (see page 30).

On the other hand, you can probably do a fair to middling job of concealing with colored wax as discussed on page 31.

BLACK SPOTS AND RINGS

The black spots I refer to are spots, and often rings, that are seen on the tops of tables and that penetrate the wood as if they were stains or black ink. They are actually discolorations of the wood caused by water, usually a sweating vase. They are the same sort of stain one sees on wooden station wagons and the varnished cabins of boats.

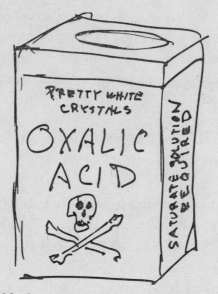

The magic black-spot remover, available in any good paint store.

The cure for this discoloration is oxalic acid, a white crystal (like salt) that you can buy in one-pound boxes in *good* paint stores. You pour these crystals into a cup of hot water until no more of them will dissolve and you see some of them undissolved in the bottom of the cup. About three rounded tablespoonfuls of the crystals will bring you to that point.

Just drip or brush this solution onto the black marks and they will disappear in seconds. Then wipe the surface a few times with a damp cloth and let the wood dry. Oxalic acid will not damage any finish.

2. Instant Refinishing

Find your ailment in this chapter. For each case a treatment is prescribed. Diagnosis: hazy, blushed, or cloudy finish . . . crackled, cracked, or alligator finish . . . worn and thin finish . . . abused ("really beat-up") finish. Treatment: abrasion, overcoating, reamalgamation, padding. A special note about Danish Modern (or any other furniture with a "sealer" finish).

AS I explained in the preface to this book, I stumbled across Instant Refinishing as a golden path to the fast buck. My idea of a fast buck is making around twenty dollars in two hours, which to me is Instant. Now, I have seen people take a week to refinish a piece of furniture that could be taken care of in two hours. They take a day to strip it, a day to stain it (drying has to go on between each operation) , a day to seal it, a day to varnish it, and two *more* days for drying. To my way of thinking, reducing the work of seven days to two hours is Instant-izing.

Of course, I have to make one provision. The Instant methods apply only to the kinds of furniture that people ordinarily have in their houses. That is to say, wooden furniture that has been stained and then covered with a clear finish of varnish, lacquer, shellac, or sealer.

What it doesn't apply to is some old table that you picked up at a junk shop that has eight coats of paint on it. Or even one coat. Instant Refinishing applies only to furniture with a clear finish—not to anything painted. This leaves us, as I say, with most of the furniture that people have in their houses: dining-room sets, hi-fi sets, sideboards, cocktail tables, bureaus, beds, chests, desks, chairs.

Now, there are several methods that can be used to perform Instant Refinishing, and the method we choose depends upon what is the matter with the piece. So I guess the best way to start out is with a listing of the conditions that need correcting, indicate the treatments for the respective conditions, then go into detail on the treatments.

DIAGNOSIS

Hazy, blushed, or cloudy finish. Here I'm talking about finishes that have a film ranging from the faintest pale gray to pure, opaque white. This condition is usually caused by moisture in the air. Pieces that have turned pure white have usually been rained on. The whiter the film, the deeper it penetrates the finish. The cure: for the lighter films, Abrasion, page 44; for pure white or halfway to it, to the point where you have to strain to see the grain of the wood, a stronger treatment is needed: Reamalgamation, page 51.

Crackled, cracked, or alligatored finish. The condition described can range from the finest hairline cracking, either widely separated or close together, to a roughness suggestive of an alligator's back. It is caused by heat—from the sun's rays or some other source. The only cure is Reamalgamation, page 51.

Worn and thin finish. I am referring here to the damage that a table top will get in ordinary usage. Typically, the surface of the finish will be scuffed or dull in the areas of heaviest use. There will be some fine surface scratches, and spots that go through to the wood. There will even be very small pit marks, which are minute dents in the finish where pieces of silverware have been dropped on the surface. The cure is simply to apply, after correct preparation, a new finish onto the old one. The prescribed treatment is called Overcoating, page 48.

Abused finish. By abused finish I mean "really beat-up." It is badly worn. Scratches are deep and even penetrate the surface of the finish entirely. There is real pockmarking, little chips having been taken out of the finish. The finish may still remain in the little dents, but it has flaked, as it will do at the edges of scratches.

For the cure, we pull the cutest of our tricks out of the bag, Padding, page 55. This is the wonder process that professional house-to-house finishers use all the time, even on slightly worn surfaces. But there are two reasons why the amateur should reserve it only for surfaces that are in bad shape. The first reason is that you are going to have to practice it for an hour or two on some surface that is of no importance before you start on a piece that you value. The second reason is that the "juice" you use in padding cannot be bought in any ordinary paint store, and you have to send away for it.

And, finally, I should mention that padding is usually considered a grown man's job. You have to rub pretty hard and keep it up for ten or fifteen minutes at a time. Of course, I'll admit that my wife can do it, but as I've always said, who wants a weak wife?

TREATMENT

Assuming that you have read the previous pages, so that we are both using my terms for the different things that can happen to furniture finishes, we can get down to what you can do about these conditions. And we will take them up in the following order: Abrasion, Overcoating, Reamalgamation, and Padding. This order is based on increasing difficulty of the techniques. All but the first one have to be practiced first on a surface that you don't particularly care about. Just one practice session with each technique will be enough. And if fifteen minutes of practice seems like an imposition, try to keep the benefits in mind: surfaces that look like new in fifteen minutes to half an hour! When, by old-fashioned refinishing methods, they would take you days.

ABRASION (For lightly hazy, blushed, or cloudy finish)

To most people, the idea of scraping the top off a furniture finish sounds crazy. They think of finishes, whether they be shellac, lacquer, or varnish, as being too thin to fool around with that way. But finishes aren't all that thin. They are about a fiftieth of an inch thick—and pretty tough.

In fact, that is the whole point. They are so tough that hazing or blushing usually penetrates only through the top five percent of the finish. And there is a perfectly safe way of removing that spoiled surface so that the ninety-five percent of the finish looks like new—fine steel wool. Grade ooo is best. Finer grades can be used—such as oooo or ooooo—but you will have to rub a lot harder and longer. In no case is sandpaper recommended. No matter how careful you are with even the finest emery paper, there is too much danger of cutting through the finish into the wood below. And if you do that, you have ruined any hopes of Instant Refinishing. Unless you are an expert toucher-up, you are going to end up by having to sand the whole finish off, restain, seal, recoat with shellac, varnish, or lacquer, and after the surface is dry, polish with steel wool and wax. So are we straight on that? NO SANDPAPER!

Also, no pumice or rottenstone should be used. These can fool you even faster than sandpaper will. They are abrasive powders that you mix with water or oil to polish the surface of finishes. But the only places they are used are in factories; and *they* make mistakes once in awhile too.

So now we have a mahogany piano, or whatever, whose top and sides are covered with a gray film that no amount of waxing or polishing will remove. The procedure is as follows:

1. The surface has to be cleaned of any wax or oil-

base polish that has been put on it over the years. There
are many ways of doing this, but only one correct, safe,
sure, and easy way. That is to go down to the hardware
store and buy a pint or a quart (a quart is enough
for a piano or dining-room table and four chairs) of
mineral spirits. This is also called paint thinner. It is
not turpentine, but a substitute costing about half as
much. For this purpose, turpentine is not better just
because it costs more.

Now take a small rag—an old washrag is ideal—and

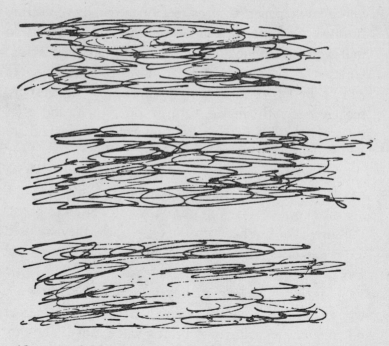

*Always unfold a pad of steel wool and tear it into three
pieces. (Isn't this the greatest illustration you've ever seen?
I worked on it a week.)*

apply the mineral spirits freely, rubbing the surface well. Now wipe off with a clean rag.

If any obvious pieces of glop remain on the surface, they must be water soluble, because the mineral spirits take off everything else. So remove them with a rag and water. For chunks of old lollipop, use a "Good Humor" stick or something like that.

2. Take a pad of ooo steel wool and unroll it. Divide it into three pieces. Using up one piece at a time, rub hard at that film. Rub in straight strokes that follow the grain of the wood. In corners, where you have to, you can rub across the grain, but try to go over those areas as much as you can with grain-following strokes to match the major area.

Always follow the grain when "rubbing down" a finish with steel wool.

After you have rubbed a portion of the surface with
five to eight strokes, wet the surface with mineral spirits
so that you can see how things are coming along. In all
likelihood most of the finish will be clear, but some
hazy areas will still be there. Rub these some more with
your wet pad of steel wool (keep applying the mineral
spirits as they evaporate) until the whole finish is clear.

3. Wipe off the piece with a dry rag, and wax your
"like-new" finish with Yankee Wax or some other good
brand of paste wax. Clean up, pack your kit, get the
lady of the house to sign your job ticket, and get out of
the house.

OVERCOATING (For worn, thin, and worn-through finishes)

What we are talking about is actually applying a new
finish—fast—over an old one. When a finish gets worn, it
isn't thick enough anymore to use the Abrasion technique. Also, in bad cases, you will have spots that are
worn through to the wood, and these must be touched
up before applying our new finish. Let's say, then, that
we have a dining-room table in scuffed condition and
that in one spot the finish has been worn down to the
bare wood.

1. Clean the whole surface with mineral spirits and
water when necessary as outlined in the section on Abrasion (page 44).

2. The area that is worn through to the wood is the

first problem. It is probably going to have to be stained
a little to match the rest of the top. Now, the professional always has a set of alcohol stains with him. These
come in powder form and when mixed with alcohol
have the advantage of drying out in about thirty seconds. But you can do just as well with a set of artist's
oil paints, the only disadvantage being that the stain you
mix with them will take about an hour to dry.

Don't protest that you never saw oil paints dry in an

SPRAY _YES!_   BRUSH _NO!_

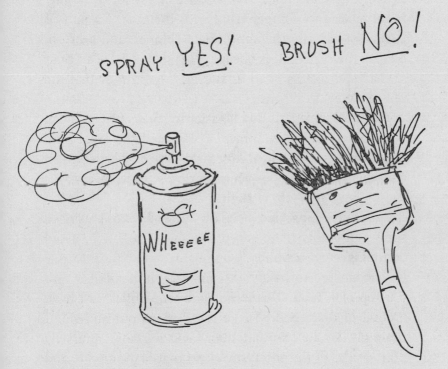

Old Yanqui refinishers go home! Viva Villa! Viva Allende!
The Revolution Lives!

hour. We are going to make such a thin wash, using no oil, that it will dry in an hour, especially if you blow on it a lot. Or if you really are in a big hurry, you can dry the stain in five minutes with an electric iron set very low and resting on a cloth, but it is safer to wait an hour if you are new at the game.

Now this is the day of the spray bomb, and the time has come to put brushes and cans of shellac and varnish behind you forever. Don't tell me they are too expensive, because they are not. One $1.69 can will do a dining-room table. Just compare that with the cost of a pint of shellac or varnish, the appropriate thinner, and a brush. So (1) the spray can is cheaper. (2) It is far better than shellac and just as good as the factory finishes that are put on new furniture.

On top of this, it is much easier to spray than to brush a finish on, and most sprays, if you read the labels, are completely dry in ten minutes. At which point you can give them a light wipe-over with ooo steel wool, wax, or polish, and the job is done.

The only thing that needs to be said about using a spray can is that there is a procedure to follow to avoid "curtains" or "pebbling."

The surface to be sprayed must be horizontal. With the top of a table, this is no problem. But if you have a chest of drawers, first take the drawers out and stand them on the floor so that their faces are horizontal. To do the sides of the chest, turn it so that first one side and then the other is horizontal.

When you do a table top, spray the edges first—including the ones that you get at by putting the leaves down. Then raise the leaves and spray the top from side to side, moving away from your edge to the far edge. In this way the liquid finish will go on evenly. If you work from the far edge to yourself, the wind from the can may hit the area you have just sprayed in your last cross stroke and cause uneven drying, resulting in dull spots.

Finally, check the edges for curtains or dripping, and you will find that it is very easy to wipe them smooth with your fingertip.

The final step, of course, is to wipe the top with ooo steel wool in smooth, even strokes that follow the grain of the wood, and then apply wax or polish.

REAMALGAMATION (For cracked, chipped, or alligatored finishes, and heavy film)

Reamalgamating is so easy that I have a hard time convincing people of it without finding an old sunbaked, weather-beaten piece and giving a demonstration. But the simple fact is that all factory-applied finishes are sprayed-on lacquer. And in almost any paint or hardware store you can buy a clear liquid that smells like nail polish and is called lacquer thinner. Lacquer thinner (besides being the solvent used in nail polish) will redissolve the lacquer coating on factory-finished furniture no matter how bad a condition the finish is in. By dipping your brush in a bowl full of lacquer thinner, you can actually dissolve and rebrush any finish that is still at least *there*. (Sometimes finishes crumble so badly that they *fall off!*)

Reamalgamation works like magic. (I worked on this illustration in my sleep.)

This is also true of antiques, but we'll talk about them in a minute. First let us deal with all "store-boughten," factory-finished furniture made in the last forty years. That brings us from about 1925 up to yesterday. Step by step, the procedure goes like this:

Reamalgamating Factory Finishes

1. Clean the old finish with mineral spirits (paint thinner). If the cracks are deep, use a scrub brush— bristle or nylon. Wipe it with a soft rag and allow it to air-dry for five minutes. The work must be done in a

reasonably dry, heated room—or outside on nice summer days. High moisture content of the air is the thing to avoid, because finishing on damp days causes poor drying and "blushing."

2. The surface to be worked on must be horizontal and level.

3. Pour about a cup of lacquer thinner into a soup bowl.

4. Use a brand-new two-inch brush. It doesn't have to be a tapered or varnish brush. It can be just an ordinary paint brush, but a *new* one. I stress this because it seems to be impossible to teach an American how to clean a brush after having used it. It does take a good ten or fifteen minutes to clean a brush so that it can be used again.*

5. Now dip the brush in the lacquer thinner and brush the surface to be reamalgamated freely with the lacquer thinner. Not sloppily, just freely. Try to get the whole surface wet as quickly as possible. The idea is to apply a little more lacquer thinner than necessary to soften the finish to ordinary brushing consistency. This should take about half a minute, more or less, as you

* Incidentally, the way to clean a brush is first to wipe it and squeeze it out. Then rinse it in four changes of clean lacquer thinner, using about half a cup of thinner each time. Wash it in soap and water four or five times, each time working up a lather and rinsing well. This routine must be started within five minutes after you have finished using the brush, whether you were using paint, varnish, lacquer, shellac, or whatever. I know it sounds like a lot of trouble, but it's the only way.

keep brushing the surface. Then "tip-off" (make your final light, smoothing brush strokes) —and stop.

At this point the surface will look like a freshly applied coat of finish. For all intents and purposes, it is. In ten minutes to half an hour it will be dry enough to rub down with ooo or oooo steel wool to remove surface roughness, then wax or polish.

And now for antiques.

Reamalgamating Antique Finishes

1. Ninety-five percent of the *clear* finishes found on antiques will be shellac. In this case, the procedure is exactly the same as I have described for modern lacquer finishes, except that you substitute denatured alcohol for the lacquer thinner. It is obtainable at any paint store, where it is sold as a thinner for shellac. To make the alcohol work more easily and smoothly, I usually add about ten or twenty percent of lacquer thinner to it. This "soups-up" the alcohol, as the cliché goes.

About five percent of the antiques you find will have been refinished with varnish (varnish wasn't invented until about 1900). In this case, the exact procedure will be either of the following:

1. Forget it. You can't reamalgamate varnish.

2. Try Abrasion (page 44). If that doesn't work, you will just have to remove the varnish and apply a new finish from scratch.

PADDING (*The all-purpose solution to almost everything*)

Now we come to the most amazing of all of the Instant Refinisher's bag of tricks. Fundamentally, this is a process of applying a new finish over an old one with a tightly rolled pad of soft cotton cloth. But that is only the beginning of the story. In the first place, this over-finish, called *padding lacquer*, is as "instant" as you can get because the liquid actually dries as you massage it onto the surface. In the second place, the squeegee action of the pad will actually fill minor cracks and imperfections in the surface. And this includes fine checking and crackling.

In the third place, it will clear all minor cases of hazing and bloom, rendering the finish crystal clear. It will also give you a mirror finish if you want it, but you can dull the finish with ooo or oooo steel wool *immediately* after you have finished rubbing. And finally, it is the easiest finish in the world to apply once you understand that the pad must never be allowed to come to a full stop on the surface or it will stick and leave an impression of the weave of the fabric used in your pad. (The obvious safeguard is that you use a constant circular of figure-8 stroke, lifting the pad off with a quick flourish when you are finished with an area.)

With all these advantages—especially the speed—this technique is obviously the favorite of all professional door-to-door refinishers. So your first question probably is "How come I never heard of padding lacquer before?" and the second (unless you think I'm making this all up) would most likely be "Where can I get some of it?"

Well, I can't really explain why padding lacquer is such a secret. But I would guess that it is because the people who practice this craft are a terribly secretive bunch. They are the kind that think trade secrets should be kept secret.

The answer to your second question is that the easiest way to get it is to order it from the very fine mail-order catalogue put out for woodworkers by Albert Constantine & Son, Inc., 2050 Eastchester Road, Bronx, New York. You might as well send 25¢ along with your letter, because that is the cost of their catalogue—and well worth it. They also sell all kinds of cabinet woods, veneers, hardware, stains, finishes, bleaches, books—the works.

Another place where you can buy padding lacquer, as well as all other finishing supplies, is H. Behlen & Sons, 14 Christopher Street, New York, New York.

Exactly How to Do Padding (The miracle finish restorer)

Grotz's Unconditional Guarantee. Regardless of what any tight-mouthed, Old-World craftsman tells you, anyone can learn to do padding in five minutes of practice by following these directions. It is really much easier, for instance, than learning to brush on a varnish finish.

You might make your first try on the back of a chair or the side of a bureau (no need to have the surface horizontal this time), because there is the problem of learning to keep the pad in motion at all times when it is touching the finish to avoid leaving a "stick mark." Stick marks are removable, but a nuisance. (How to remove them is covered at the end of this section, but most people only let their pad get stuck once. So, do it on your practice piece to get it out of your system.)

With that word of caution, let us proceed step by step:

1. First, you make this tight pad that I have mentioned. Start with a piece of cotton about the size of two handkerchiefs. In fact, two handkerchiefs will do. Or tear a piece out of the back of a cotton shirt. There are lots of ways to make your pad, but to start with, you might as well have the best kind—that is, the easiest to handle—and for this see the illustration.

2. Now pour about a quarter of a cup of padding lacquer into a saucer, and dip your pad. Wet it thoroughly, and then squeeze it tight to remove excess liquid. Later you can wet your pad from the mouth of a five-ounce bottle; this is what we door-to-door people keep in our kits, because it is enough to do the top of a dining-room table.

3. Just relax and start stroking your surface with the pad in a figure-8 pattern. Keep dipping the pad into the padding lacquer so that you can build up a coating on the surface. Start with a gentle touch to wet the surface, but gradually increase the pressure until you are rubbing

really hard. This pressure creates the squeegee effect that forces the hardening fluid into the crevices and at the same time generates the heat that makes the lacquer dry.

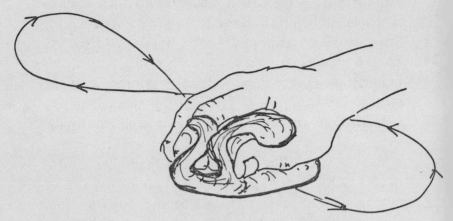

Use a figure-8 stroke in padding to avoid having your pad stick to a "hot" finish.

The figure-8 stroke is the best for covering large areas such as table tops. You have quite a lot of stroking to do. About fifteen minutes of it. But it is not the only stroke. You can use long edge-to-edge strokes, and little short ones to get into corners. Just so long as you apply and pick up your pad gradually.

4. When the whole surface is clear and smooth, you stop wetting the pad but keep rubbing to complete the drying of the coating of lacquer. If you have taken twelve or fifteen minutes to apply your coating, then keep rubbing for about four or five minutes more.

5. You will now have a mirrorlike surface. And if that is what you want, all you do is leave it overnight to dry before applying a coat of paste wax and using it.

If, however, you want a "dull glow," you can achieve it by wiping or "rubbing-down" the surface with ooo or oooo steel wool. Now, a professional, who is sure of himself, will dull the finish as soon as he has put his pad and bottle of padding lacquer away. (His pad goes into a jar to keep it clean and ready for use on his next job.) But if you are not trying to prove something, you might just go and have a cup of coffee for about half an hour. You can feel perfectly sure in that way that the whole surface is well dried.

Then you unroll your pad of steel wool, tear it into three equal parts, and stroke the surface in long strokes that follow the grain of the wood. When the surface is evenly dulled, apply a coat of paste wax, and it is ready to use. (You don't have to wait overnight if you have steel-wooled the surface to dull it.)

And that, friends and foes, is all there is to it. Except to explain what to do if you commit the error of getting your pad stuck. There are two things you can do. The professional would apply a half teaspoonful of mineral oil to the spot and then grind down the unevenness with emery paper wrapped around a small piece of flat wood. Then he would wipe this with a dry rag and resume padding right away.

For amateurs who are nervous about this procedure, a more time-consuming method is to apply padding lacquer freely with a brush, and brush out the unevenness. And then apply a coat of padding lacquer—with the brush—to the whole surface. Let this coating dry overnight, and then start all over again.

A SPECIAL NOTE ABOUT DANISH MODERN
(Or any other furniture with a "sealer" finish)

A sealer finish is one that doesn't lie on the surface as a coating but penetrates the surface of the wood and hardens there, keeping anything else from getting in. As a result, it is a very dull finish and you can usually feel the grain of the wood with your fingertips.

The point is that, no matter what may be the condition of your sealer finish (it is widely used on Danish Modern), none of the processes mentioned apply if you want to restore it but keep the same dull, zero-thickness finish. On the other hand, it is very easy to restore one of these finishes. All you have to do is get some ordinary floor sealer from your paint store. Then, after you have carefully cleaned the surface with paint thinner or turpentine, you apply a coat of sealer, letting it sink in for five or ten minutes. Then you wipe off the excess with soft rags. Let it dry twenty-four hours, apply a paste wax, and polish briskly.

If you are a mail-order type of person, a fine sealer is sold by Francis Hagerty, Cohasset Colonials, Cohasset, Massachusetts. And just for the record I should add that, if you are tired of the dullness of your sealer finish, you can spray or brush any "bodied" finish over it, such as shellac, varnish, or lacquer, and it will stay on top. For directions on how to do this, see Overcoating, page 48.

3. The "Antiqued" Finish

Maybe not Instant—but fast and easy. It's the sneaky art of Making Something Out of Nothing. Ground coat, decoration, glaze, finishing off, pickled finish.

IN the best of times or the worst of times, the French have always been able to make a lot out of a little. This is widely known about their cooking, which historically is known to be based on making slightly rotten meat and smelly fish taste delicious by the artful use of spices and sauces. But it also applies to their method of painting and glazing furniture out of a common piece of secondhand junk that will still stand up.

This process, for lack of a more honest name, is called *antiquing*. It consists of painting the piece either white or a pastel blue or green and then wiping a dark-brown-tinted glaze over it. Sometimes designs and decorations are painted on before the glaze is applied. The most famous practitioner of this art is Peter Hunt, of the charming New England town of Orleans, Massachusetts, which is about halfway out on Cape Cod.*

And if that sounds like a free plug for an old friend, that is exactly what it is. For Peter gave me my first job in this business on a very cold winter afternoon some

* He even has published a book on it, which you can find in most libraries: Peter Hunt's *How-to-do-it Book*, Prentice-Hall, 1952.

twenty-odd years ago, when he had his shop in Provincetown, on the tip of the Cape. Everyone in the trade knows and respects Peter Hunt—or "Pierre le Chasseur," as the Old Master often signs his pieces.

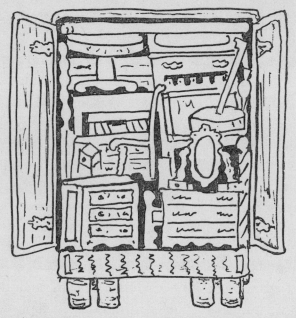

The back of Peter Hunt's fall truck from Boston. It was usually packed like a Chinese puzzle. But that's the way life is as far as I've seen it.

In those days he used to go to Boston every fall and buy up enough abandoned Victorian furniture—oak and walnut—to fill a trailer truck, and I mean packed in like a Chinese puzzle. A lot of this had to be stripped down before the ground coat of paint, the decorations, and the glaze could be applied—and guess who was

assigned to the stripping-down department in an un-
heated cellar. Little old me, that's who. But when
spring came, and the redecorated furniture was being
shipped out to the best department stores across the
country, I could say to myself, "And where would Peter
Hunt be without me?"

To get to the point, anyone who can wield a paint
brush can turn the worst "dog" into an attractive and
even sophisticated piece of furniture. It isn't one of
those things you have to be very careful about; your
mistakes will actually add "character" to the piece—
brush marks or chips in the finish beneath your ground
coat simply add to the texture.

Now, there are many variations of antiquing, but there
are four basic steps:

1. Applying the "ground" coat of paint.

2. Painting on the decoration, if any. This usually
consists simply of applying a different color of paint to
the knobs and edges or some striping. But if you are
something of an artist, this can range from Peter Hunt's
peasant style of decoration, through découpage, and all
the way up to poor man's trompe l'oeil—a glove hanging
out of a drawer, say, or trying to make a chest look like
a Greek temple.

3. Applying the glaze with rag or brush.

4. Finishing off the surface with wax or a coat of the
"dust of ages." This last is fake, of course, and is really
pumice or rottenstone applied in such a way as to stick
in corners and crevices.

Now, let us take up these steps or processes one at a

time with all the variations that I can think of; then you can wade in and create your own masterpiece in the manner of your choice.

GROUND COAT

"Ground coat" is a nice, professional-sounding term, but all it means is that you are going to take an old piece of furniture and paint it—and not too neatly either, because you get no points for neatness in antiquing. Junky-looking bureaus are especially rewarding, because antiqued pieces are really at their best in a girl's or woman's bedroom. Any round table, and chairs done to match, are also always good. And, of course, hope chests, boxes, cupboards, and especially those heavy Victorian chairs dripping with carving and nasty lions' heads.

When painting anything, it is, of course, best to wash the surface first with mineral spirits to remove wax. Then you pick the color of paint you want. The commonest colors are white, aqua, and pale blues and greens. You can use pink, if someone insists, though it's a little effeminate for my taste. That covers most of the colors except yellow, which does not look good under the brown glazing.

Now I have said to use pale colors, because that is the popular taste, but you have to remember that the brown glaze is going to darken things up. You can use darker tones, which will give you a richer, more serious and

Byzantine, quite sophisticated look. I remember one piece that had been done in a medium tone of bluish green. The paint had been scratched with a wire brush to give the surface a lot of texture. Then a reddish-brown glaze had been applied, and the edges of the top and the knobs of this low bureau gleamed with bronze through the glaze. It looked as if a dark, sultry brunette should have been sitting on it.

As to the kind of paint, your most likely choice is semi-gloss enamel. But I have seen people who knew just what they wanted using flat rubber-base paint as well as high-gloss enamel. Using high-gloss enamel doesn't make too much difference except that your glaze will be more streaky and stylized. With a flat paint, you will get a pretty dark effect.

DECORATION

The best-loved decorating procedure is to highlight the edges of furniture tops and the knobs on bureaus with gold, yellow, or medium-orange paint. In other words, warm colors to go against a cool ground. And that, plus your glaze and dust, will give a charming effect and is probably all you would want for living and dining rooms.

If you are the artistic type, and want to paint on decorations, use the little quarter-pint cans of enamel sold in any paint store.

For découpage, glue your cut-outs on the ground color,

and then cover the whole piece with a coat of clear shellac or spray lacquer. This will keep the glaze from soaking into the paper when you apply it. Always use a white glue.

GLAZE

Glaze is simply varnish tinted with a dead brown that is called burnt umber, which you can buy in a tube wherever you can buy the varnish. You can also try *raw* umber, which is such a dead brown that it is almost gray when thinned down. Or if you want a redder, more orange tone, you can add a *little* burnt sienna to either of the umbers. Now these choices aren't anything to get in a flap about, because you can try out a glaze on your ground color, and if you don't like it, just wipe if off with a rag dipped in mineral spirits. But for those of you who need to feel secure about this, my suggestion is to start with the burnt umber.

For the average mixing of color with varnish, start with half a tube of color to half a pint of varnish. Applying the glaze is again no worry, because if you don't like what you have, you can wipe if off with a rag dipped in mineral spirits and start all over again. The best material with which to apply the glaze is burlap, because you want the glaze to go on in a scratchy, streaky way. A piece of toweling or a washcloth is also good. Soak the glaze into the crevices and corners and then wipe it away and out onto the flat areas. There is really nothing to it,

Even without much molding, a glaze can still be effective.
(Bronze paint on knobs and edge of top.)

as you will see. For furniture tops, wipe the glaze on
the edges and then spread it toward the middle. If
you get too much glaze on, wipe off the excess with a
rough dry rag.

FINISHING OFF

After the glaze has dried thoroughly, wipe or gently
rub it down with grade ooo steel wool to smooth it, and
then apply a coat of paste wax. This is especially important on surfaces that will get use, such as table and
bureau tops. But for cupboards and anything that is
highly carved, it is a nice touch to add the "dust of
ages." The standard way to do this is to mix rottenstone
(a fine powder you can buy at any paint store) with
water until you have something of the consistency of

thin paint. Brush this on the piece freely, and then wipe if off, leaving a little of the powder in the cracks and crevices. Don't worry, it'll stay there—and your house can look just like a museum.

What we have just run through is only the classical or standard approach to glazing or antiquing. You can also use thinned-down brown, white, or black paint for your glaze. For a very feminine frosted effect, apply thinned white paint as a glaze over a pale pink or blue. You certainly don't have to follow any rules or even the method I have described, which is just to give you the general idea.

PICKLED FINISH

A first cousin to the antiqued finish is the pickled finish, which is often covered with an antiquing glaze.

A pickled finish is most successful if the wood is oak, because of its large open pores. The idea is to have these pores filled with one color of paint while the rest of the surface is stained another color. The colors most commonly used are dark green, gray, and black—with the pores filled with white paint.

To do this, first brush on a thin coat of glossy enamel paint—a thin coat so that the pores don't fill. Then, after that coat is dry, wipe flat white paint over the surface, forcing it into the pores and then wiping it off of the rest of the surface. You can also apply a glaze over the surface if you want, but you won't be able to see the glaze unless your ground color is fairly light.

4. Finishing Raw Wood

Revealing the foolproof way the experts use on unfinished furniture, built-in cabinets, and paneling: the super-easy, one-coat sealer finish.

ANYBODY can put a finish on raw wood, but there may be a few hints I can give you.

For instance, did you know that there is a trick to staining plywood so that it doesn't end up looking like a flat zebra? What you do, *before* you stain it, is to give it a coat of thinned-down shellac (one-half shellac and one-half denatured alcohol). When this is dry, rub down the whole surface with ooo steel wool to smooth the surface and remove some of the shellac from the hard streaks in the grain. Of course, the shellac has sunk into the soft areas, where it will block the stain from sinking in. So now, when you apply your stain, you will have a much more even coloring. If you really want to fake out, apply two coats of shellac, rubbing down each coat with steel wool. Then, if you wipe on a pigmented oil stain, you can make plywood look like almost anything. (To get your stain stronger, pour about half the clear liquid off the top of the can before stirring up the pigment in the bottom.)

Incidentally, this primer coat of shellac is the secret of getting a good paint job on unfinished wood, whether it be plywood or the nicest even-grained pine, as is usually found in unfinished furniture. You'll be amazed how smoothly paint goes on to a surface that has previously been sealed with shellac and then rubbed down with ooo steel wool. (I know that the paint companies tell you that you can't do this, but you and I know better.)

The important fact about unfinished pine furniture is that the easiest and best-looking treatment is to give it a one-coat, wipe-on sealer finish. Now, the fellow in the paint store will tell you that he hasn't any sealer finish for furniture—just for floors. Well, they are exactly the same thing. And if he doesn't have the color you want, simply buy a pint of clear sealer, squeeze a thirty-five-cent tube of oil stain into it, and stir well.

The tubes of color are the same ones used for tinting paints, and the colors you are interested in are the two siennas (raw and burnt) and the two umbers (raw and burnt). These are called the earth colors, and by mixing them you can obtain almost any wood color you want. You might also need a very little orange for a maple color. Stay away from red. Red is always *too* red, and you'll be sorry in the end that you used it at all.

Now you have your sealer—either bought colored or colored by you—and that means that the hardest part of the job is already over (parting with the cash, that is). Sealer is so easy to use, with "perfect results every time," that eight-year-olds can master it.

All you have to do is brush it freely onto the wood. Or mop it on or put it on with a rag, or even squish it on with your bare hands. Apply it freely until it stops sinking into the wood and some traces remain on the surface for ten minutes after you applied the last coat. Then wipe off the excess with rags or paper towels and let the wood dry overnight (or, say, for four hours in a warm, dry room).

When the wood is dry, rub it down with ooo steel wool to smooth the surface, and wax it with a good paste wax. You will then have as serviceable a finish as any in the world—for eating meals off of, for a cocktail table, or whatever.*

* This book is about fast and easy ways of finishing and refinishing furniture. For the hard and long ways, see my book *The Furniture Doctor*, $4.95, Doubleday & Company, 1962, available through any bookstore. (*Good* bookstores even keep it in stock.) That book goes into all kinds of involved things like mixing stains, varnishing, bronze stenciling, making repairs—the works.

5. Refinishing Antiques — Instantly and Otherwise

Some extra hints and asides on those treasures you found in Grandma's attic—or more likely in the local Salvation Army store.

THROUGH most of this book we have been talking about old furniture—say ten or twenty or even forty years old. Or furniture that is not so old but has had some rough times. (Why is it that little kids hate furniture so?) But there seems to be a big thing in this country about *antique* furniture, which you can date from the Victorian Era, ending around 1900. Some people even include the Golden Oak of the early 1900s. And while all the techniques I've written about in this book apply to antiques also, there are some special points about them that are worth a little of our attention.

Now, we'll get down to cases in a minute, but first let's discuss a little of the theory of antiques—at least, the way I see it. What I mean is that you don't own antiques for the same reasons that you own regular furniture. There are two possibilities:

1. You have them to impress people—with your taste, sophistication, ancestors, or whatever.

2. You have them because you enjoy old things. You find charm in their hand work, their functional design, the integrity of their solid construction. They unques-

tionably do represent and remind us of everything that is best in our American heritage. They are pieces of history brought into the present. Each style represents an era in our growth as a nation and the kind of men and women who lived in earlier times—Colonial, expansion in the early 1800s, Civil War, the rush and excitement of Victorian times. To know the styles and stories and men and great events of the past is to know your origins and to be able to know better where you are and who you are right now.

And that leads us into the fundamental thing about refinishing or restoring antiques: Their being old and *looking* old is the whole point. Sure, you want an antique to look clean and the grain of the wood to show. But you also want to preserve the signs of wear and usage that give the piece its individual character and set it apart from a factory-perfect reproduction. There is also the fact that, as wood ages, its surface darkens and achieves a soft patina that cannot be duplicated in any factory.

All right, you say, and just how do we go about performing this feat of making old wood look as good as new, only still old?

The answer is that from this day forward you will turn your back on sandpaper. Ah, the sandpaper of your youth—the bright new pieces, the grubby little bits that were just enough to round the front of a balsawood airplane model before you painted—yes, it must leave your life and be put out of mind forever. In its place, think of steel wool, nice, fine, gentle steel wool.

Let us, for example, say that you have just wheedled an heirloom out of Grandma or sneaked one out of the dump or bought one from a junkman. How do you start, and what do you do?

Well, the first thing you do is to set your piece up in a room with windows in it so that even in winter you can open them to let the fumes out. Then make some provision to protect the floor if it is worth protecting. Now you assemble—preferably on a small work table— the following materials:

1. Some rags.

2. A soup bowl.

3. An old nylon fingernail brush (not absolutely necessary, but useful).

4. A package (16 pads) of grade 1 or 0 steel wool. This is pretty coarse and from here on will be called the "rough" steel wool. (You'll probably use only three pads of this, but it is always useful to have some left over for the next time you get ambitious.)

5. A package of ooo steel wool, which I'll refer to as the "fine" steel wool.

6. One quart of lacquer thinner (from paint store).

7. One quart of denatured alcohol (formerly called "wood alcohol" and also from paint store).

Now you might have noticed that you have just put paint remover behind you. The reason is not that it would destroy the patina of old wood. It is just that the retail price of paint and varnish removers is ridiculously high. (See the following chapter on cheap substitutes.) And denatured alcohol and lacquer thinner remove the old finishes just as well and much faster, because you do not have to worry about washing off the paint-remover residue or, in the case of water-rinse removers, letting the piece dry before applying a new finish. You can put a new finish on as soon as the old one is off. As a result, even major pieces such as desks, chests, and large tables can be refinished in two or three hours if you use one of our "instant" finishing techniques such as Overcoating (page 48) or Padding (page 55).

The reason that this speed-up is possible is that denatured alcohol and lacquer thinner are not actually removers but are solvents of the old finishes. They dissolve the dirty old finish, and you just wipe it away. Also, both these solvents are so volatile that traces of them left on the wood after wiping the finish off will evaporate completely in thirty seconds. That's a lot faster than you will be able to prepare to put your new finish on.

To spell this out for you, let's say you are lucky enough to have a cherry drop-leaf table.

1. First, slop about a quarter of a cup of each of the solvents on the top of the table to see which works better. Usually they work about the same, but once in awhile one does and the other doesn't. Sometimes they work best when mixed together. Try and find out. I usually just fill my bowl with about half of each and go to work.

2. Do the top first. Pour your solvent into the bowl until it is about half full. Holding it next to the table, slop the solvent on with a pad of your coarse steel wool. Coat the whole top, and keep applying more

until you have a great gooey mess. You can soak up most of this by using your pad of steel wool like a sponge and squeezing the gunk into an old tin can. I don't wear gloves, but ladies prefer to.

When most of the gunk is off the surface, finish up by wiping the surface with pieces of cloth dipped in your solvent bowl.

3. A good way to do the legs is to stand them one at a time right in your bowl of solvent, which, of course, you keep refilling. Just slop the finish up the legs with your rough steel wool or an old brush, and wash the old finish down into the bowl. The brush comes in handy here for carved legs.

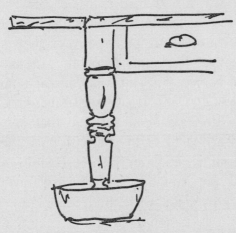

Bowl or dishpan. Put the leg of the table into the solution when removing paint from it. Messy, but economical!

4. To do the ends of the table, tip it up. The same goes for doing the sides of chests. It's always easier to work on a comparatively level surface.

Now here is a bonus. After you have finished giving the table a final wipe-down, it not only is immediately ready for a new finish, it already has a base finish because the residue of the old finish is left in the pores of the wood. This means that you now need only one coat of new finish, whereas you would need two if you had used a paint and varnish remover. (And, as I mentioned before, with a water-rinse remover you would have had drying time to boot.)

A beautifully quick and attractive way to finish the job now is to spray it with a can of clear, quick-drying spray. Let that dry a few minutes, wipe it down with your fine steel wool, and apply a coat of boiled linseed oil, which you rub off hard with clean rags after a few minutes. The boiled linseed oil will give you the dull glow that connoisseurs prefer on antiques, and it will even make the piece smell good—the way old furniture should. Of course, you can wax your new finish if you want a higher shine (see Overcoating, page 48).

Now, in the case of an antique that has been desecrated with one to eight coats of paint, we have to throw all our ideas about Instant Refinishing out the window. There isn't any fast or easy way to remove paint. But there are ways, and some are easier than others. For a discussion of this pesky subject, see the following chapter and learn how to be a paint remover.

6. Inexpensive Paint Removers

An irrelevant but useful bonus chapter about the "secret" chemicals you can use to make cheap paint removers, and inside information on setting up your own dipping tank—which is a lot easier and cheaper than you think. That old debbil lye . . . ammonia . . . trisodium phosphate.

I KNOW that the subject of cheap paint removers doesn't have much to do with Instant Refinishing, but it burns me up to have to pay six or seven dollars for a gallon of paint remover that I know cost the manufacturer about fifty-five cents to make. I could understand it if they advertised paint remover on television, because then we would be paying for the commercials. I'm not the only one that's baffled, because people are always asking me if I know any secret ways to get paint off cheaply and easily.

Well, there isn't any easy way (except to pay somebody to do the job for you), but there are a number of cheap ways that have been figured out. So here is a collection of the ones that I have tried over the years and found to work. Everybody in the antique business has used them at one time or another. The materials are lye, ammonia, and trisodium phosphate. These are listed in the order of their commonest availability. You can buy the first two in any supermarket, and we'll discuss finding the last one as we get to it.

That Old Debbil Lye

Probably the most widely used solution of all is lye, because it will work when all else fails, including some of the manufactured paint removers. It is especially effective when there are many layers of paint. Let's say you have a dining-sized table with eight layers of paint on it. You could easily use up two gallons of store-bought paint remover getting this off and it would cost you from ten to fifteen dollars. With lye, the cost would be around a dollar. And it is faster.

But there are two drawbacks to lye. The first is that you have to use it outside the house so that you can wash the piece off with a garden hose. The second is that lye will only work in warm weather, when the temperature of the air is over 70 degrees. The warmer it is, the better. So you can't use lye at all times of the year. You have to wait for a fairly warm summer day—unless you have a heated barn or cellar with a built-in drain or dirt floor to take away the water from your garden hose.

But let's say you have the proper temperature, a garden hose, and either a drainage system or a spot of lawn where you don't mind if the grass doesn't grow too well for a couple of years. (Lye doesn't do grass *any* good at all!) This, then, is your working procedure:

1. Assemble the following materials:

A tin or enameled pail.

A pair of rubber gloves, preferably the heavier kind, lined with cloth.

Someplace where you don't care if the grass ever grows again.

Two cans of lye crystals, which are commonly sold in supermarkets for cleaning drains. Sometimes the lye comes under trade names, but they always make it fairly obvious what is in the cans. Lycons is one well-known name.

An applicator to use in applying the lye solution to the paint. A small dish-mop is good, but hard to find these days. Old paint brushes aren't any good, because the lye dissolves the bristles. I usually wire a piece of rag to the end of a two-foot stick.

2. Now it is time to make up your lye solution, and here is where many people go wrong, because they make the solution too weak. The *right* mixture is one can of lye to one quart of water. It might work if it is made a little weaker, but with the price of a can of lye so low this is no time to be a cheapskate. And don't worry about the lye "burning the wood." It does turn some woods very dark, but there is a quick and easy solution to that, which I'll discuss later.

Two cans of lye and two quarts of water will be enough for most pieces of furniture. A big hutch cabinet might take four cans and four quarts.

Important: Put the water in the pail first. Then sprinkle the lye crystals into the water. If you put the water on top of the lye, the solution will boil up and spatter.

3. Dip your mop into the lye-water solution and apply it to the paint. As the paint dissolves, keep applying more solution until you are down to the bare wood. For getting paint out of cracks, use a wire brush, a putty knife, or a paint scraper.

4. Wash the dissolved paint off with water. The garden hose is best, but I suppose you can do it with pails of water if you can organize your friends into a bucket brigade.

5. Wipe the whole piece dry with rags, and then

Well, you're not supposed to drink it!

brush it over with vinegar to neutralize any traces of the lye that remain on the surface or in crevices. (If any lye is left on the wood, it will prevent your finish from drying properly.) Rinse the whole piece off again, wipe it dry with rags, and you are done. Before you can apply a finish to a piece stripped this way, you should let it dry for three days in a normally heated room.

Now a final word on lye. In most cases a lye solution

will turn wood (pine, for instance) a beautiful antique brown, which is perfect for most antiques. But if for any reason you want a lighter color, substitute Clorox or any other liquid laundry bleach for the vinegar rinse. Clorox will neutralize the lye as well as the vinegar will, and it will also bleach the wood back to its lightest natural shade. The Clorox will still do this even after the piece has dried out. And in that case, after bleaching you have only to wipe the surface down with wet rags. Thorough rinsing isn't needed.

Ammonia

A problem you are likely to encounter with antique furniture is that it sometimes has an old coat of paint on it. The answer is ammonia. Professionals use it, because it will cut old paint when other removers have failed. With antique furniture, milk paint is the culprit. Milk paint is the catch-all name for the dry bottom coat sometimes found on antiques, especially pine cabinets and chests. Milk was almost always used, but in various combinations with blood and colored clays, and no oil base. Milk paint is practically a thin coating of stone, and I have never heard of a paint remover that bothers it in the least. But ammonia, used straight from the bottle, will cut right through it in a minute or two.

Incidentally, before you go about destroying a coat of milk paint, you should remember that it has a great value of its own. It shouldn't be removed if it's in good condition. A pine lift-top commode, for instance, with a good milk-paint finish (usually a dull red) would be worth almost twice as much as the same chest in a clear finish. (You can see some beautiful examples in the museum houses in Old Sturbridge Village, Sturbridge, Massachusetts.)

Anyhow, the way to use ammonia on this finish is to apply it straight from the bottle with a mop or an old brush, or even a pad of rough steel wool. Swirl it around until the paint dissolves to a thin paste. Rinse this off with water and let the piece dry.

Generally speaking, the ammonia treatment will cause pine, poplar, and the fruit woods to take on a pleasing antique brown. But with cherry, mahogany, and oak the darkening is so pronounced that you will probably want to bleach the wood.

If you decide to keep the dark brown tone, whatever the wood, simply let the piece dry thoroughly (twenty-four hours at least) and then apply your finish. This should be shellac (bought fresh) thinned to a fifty-fifty mixture with denatured alcohol (also bought fresh). You can use a spray can of shellac, instead, which is thinned enough already. After this is dry, rub down with your fine steel wool and apply a second coat. This top coat should be a spray varnish, available at any good paint store.

If you don't want to keep the dark tone after the ammonia treatment, you can readily bleach out the brown with any household laundry bleach, such as Clorox, as I explain on page 92. (If you read the fine print—and I mean really fine—you will see that the active ingredient in all the bleaches is the same: sodium hypochlorite. This chemical is so cheap that it should cost about a nickel a quart—but then we have to pay for all those television commercials.)

After bleaching, rub the surface gently with a wet rag and wipe dry. After twenty-four hours, finish as I have explained.

In working with ammonia, you are going to have a terrible problem with fumes if you work indoors. The fumes can knock you out if you are with them long enough in a confined space. You have to use ammonia out of doors or in front of a window, with the fan pumping the fumes out of the room.*

T.s.p.—or trisodium phosphate

T.s.p. is the active ingredient in many detergents, and people caught on to its being a paint remover back when Spic & Span first came out, with about twice as much t.s.p. in it as it has now. It sometimes used to remove paint when you were just trying to wash your woodwork with it.

Of course, it is much better to use straight t.s.p., which can be bought from companies who sell soaps and

---

* Bonus formula: did you know you can make spirits of ammonia by filling a small bottle half full of cloves and filling it up with half water and half regular household ammonia? A doctor told me.

detergents to laundries. These are listed under "Laundry Suppliers" in the Yellow Pages of your telephone book. Such companies exist only in cities of some size or in centrally located distribution cities.

T.s.p. is very cheap, usually ten or twelve cents a pound in small quantities, about $8.50 for a hundred-pound bag. To use it in small quantities, you make a saturated solution: to a gallon of hot water add as much of the powder as will dissolve in it. This will be a little less than three cupfuls. Use this solution in the same way as I described in the discussion on lye (page 90).

T.s.p. is not as strong as lye when used this way. You do have to use gloves, but it won't give you the same kind of scalding burn that lye will on bare skin. A man with tough hands can even put his fingers in it for a few seconds at a time if he rinses them right away. But the stuff does work. It is, in fact, the chemical that is used in dipping tanks by antique dealers. These tanks will strip a whole chest in five minutes, because the solution in them is heated, and when a t.s.p. solution is hot—say, one hundred and fifty degrees or hotter—it works fast. And no neutralizing is necessary—just a thorough rinsing with water is sufficient. Nor will t.s.p. darken the wood the way lye does. Sometimes it darkens slightly, but not much. And this can be bleached out with your liquid laundry bleach.